LET'S INVESTIGATE

KEEPING FIT

ph

Published in this edition by Peter Haddock Ltd, Pinfold Lane,
Bridlington, East Yorkshire YO16 5BT

© 1997 Peter Haddock Ltd/Geddes & Grosset Ltd

ISBN 0 7105 0983 9

Printed and bound in India

PART ONE

UNDERSTANDING FITNESS
Fitness for life

Fitness is a glorious feeling of well-being. It can mean the ability to work hard, to play hard, to perform well in sports. It is the ability to use every moment of the day productively and wake up the next morning refreshed and relaxed. It means different things to different people; the fitness of the ordinary person going to work, gardening, washing the car; the fitness of the top footballer and athlete, the swimmer and climber; the fitness of the boy and girl at school. Man could not get to the moon until the astronauts had prepared themselves by hard physical training. During the flight they exercised as well as they could to maintain their fitness. All human animals require muscular exercise. If you cannot obtain this exercise you will not grow and develop properly. As you get older you must be fit to take part in hard sports; when still older you must try to stay physically active to avoid some heart troubles and to prevent the stiffness that often comes with old age. The habits of physical exercise must be started when young. To stay fit requires an effort, and this effort must be part of your life.

Keep a diary

Keep a diary for a week of all the physical activity you take. Include walking to school, playing in the playground, physical education lessons, sports activities. Compare your diary with that of friends. See what conclusions you can draw from the facts. If your friends seem fitter is it because they walk to school or cycle, or go swimming regularly?

Study your family. Do your parents exercise? Who takes the dog for a walk? Find out how top sporting figures train. How do pop stars and politicians keep fit? What fitness training did the astronauts do before being able to withstand the stresses of their journey to the moon?

Make a newsbook on the subject of fitness and have different pages for athletes, politicians and other groups of well-known people.

THE RIGHT FOOD

Not only must you exercise but you must eat the right foods. To be fat, really fat, is not healthy. Boys and girls, men and women, like to have a pleasing shape. We cannot all have the same shape; some are fatter, others more muscular, and some are bonier. Later in this book we will study these differences. To avoid being over-fat

you should eat less of foods that have a high content of sugar and fat. You should eat more protein and fresh fruit and vegetables. As a general rule, you will get fat only if you eat more food than is necessary for your individual needs. Food is turned into energy that you use to go about your daily life. Study and play at school both need energy. The manual worker needs more than the clerk. Some people need a lot of food and stay slim; others eat little but find it difficult not to become fat. Scientists are constantly studying eating habits in an effort to help everyone remain healthy.

Project

A week's food

Make a note of all the food you eat in a week. Ask your teachers (biology, physical education, health education) which foods are fattening, which are specially good for bones and teeth. Why are raw vegetables better than over-cooked ones? What are vitamins and mineral salts? Why is whole-wheat bread better than white? Brown sugar better than refined white? Honey better than both? How can you improve your diet? What is a balanced diet? Why is garlic a good medicine? Why are artificially sweetened drinks bad? Find out all you can about food, drink and diet. Why tobacco, alcohol and drugs can be dangerous to health. Find out all you can about the environment and how it affects our state of health.

When you have found the answers to the questions, make a chart of the foods you need to keep fit. The foods you like to eat, but must not eat too much. And those that you should cut out of your diet.

GOOD HABITS

Physical activity can help you stay slim and be more relaxed. It will keep you full of vitality, give tone to your muscles, and may keep you looking and feeling younger for a longer time. Good eating and sleeping habits, positive attitudes to other people, and satisfying hobbies, will all help to keep you *fit* for life. Keeping fit in the fresh air is particularly healthy. Healthy people do *not* usually need medicines, drugs and tablets.

Before trying to get fit, you should ensure that your health is generally good. If you are at all worried, do not take part in vigorous exercise until you have seen your doctor.

Warning: in this little book you will be introduced to hundreds of interesting ideas for fitness training. *Do not try them all at once.* After you have read the book you might find one or two ideas that suit you. Start with them and do not switch to others until you have given your first choice a good try.

Reporting fitness

Study television and newspapers, and note when and how they mention fitness. Suggest how they could improve their coverage. Write to them if you have any bright ideas. Start a fitness campaign in your family. Keep a diary for a *before and after* study.

Ask your teacher to show videos on diet and fitness training. Some are made by commercial firms who are interested in sport, others by government agencies. Make a list of all films and videos you can find.

FITNESS AND HEALTH

Some people might tell you that you cannot say exactly what physical fitness is. Perhaps not, but you know well what it is not. Similarly, they say that there is no proof that fitness training makes you healthy. Ask them for the proof that it does not. If you *feel* better you will *be* better. Let the doubters find proof to show that your inspired guess is wrong!

But there is some evidence to show that physical exercise helps in many conditions. It can help people to avoid heart troubles in middle age. It can help older people to delay some of the effects of ageing. Asthma and bronchitis might be helped by exercise. Obesity can be partially controlled by physical effort. Remedial physical exercise helps thousands of sick people to get back to work more quickly. Of course being fit does not stop you getting infectious diseases.

Fitness and sport help you meet other people, to find friends with similar interests, and help the whole family to do something together. Without sport how else would schools make contact with each other? Sports groups learn how to behave to each other in groups, shaking hands, lining up to clap the opposition, accepting the referee's decision, taking defeat well and being a modest winner. All this is also fitness—personality and character fitness.

When you decide to take up a fitness training programme you must be well disciplined, decide on something special and stand by your decision. In other words you learn how to make decisions about life. You must decide against tobacco and alcohol and other drugs if you want to be really healthy. You must also choose moderation, not fanaticism. Begin to think of the time available to you and how to make a time budget, not only for fitness but for all aspects of life and leisure. Through the physical effort you undertake, you will get to know your weaknesses and your strengths. You will win the respect of others, and find that physical effort can help balance your life against other stresses and strains. It helps you to unwind and relax.

Project 🔍

Time budget clock

Draw a circle and divide it into sections of different colours to show how much time you spend each day on different activities. The circle is a clock with 24 hours marked. Say 8 hours are taken by sleep and 8 hours by work. This leaves 8 hours for other activities. Detail them carefully. How many for family duties, travelling, shopping, playing, for watching television or playing computer games? See how much time you have left for personal fitness and if you can improve your use of it. Compare your time budget clock with those of your friends and your family. You might all learn from it.

List all the books you can find about fitness and health. Ask your local librarian to suggest titles.

From your newspaper see how many inches of

newsprint are given each week to health and compare it with sport, education and politics. Read your weekly or monthly magazines and study the advice sections on health. These can go in your newsbook. Do not be afraid to write for advice yourself.

HOLIDAYS

Holidays offer a chance to spend more time than usual keeping fit. On holiday, the whole family can walk, run, climb, play, swim and relax. But it is no good exercising with great enthusiasm on holiday and then forgetting to continue with fitness training during the rest of the year.

Some fitness training for lifting and handling heavy objects will keep you out of hospital, because many back problems are caused by bad lifting techniques. As a

general rule keep the back straight and use the legs for lifting. Keep heavy weights near the centre of the body.

Negative health is absence of sickness; positive health means being physically, mentally and socially fit.

Project

A holiday diary

Keep a diary on your next holiday and at the end see how much physical activity you have taken. Compare it with the amount you normally take. Compare your weight before and after. Ask yourself if you feel better.

See how many definitions of health and fitness you can find. Compare them and see if they have any points in common.

Map all the possible walks in the country near your home; or in the parks if you live in a city. If you do live in the heart of the city find out how much it would cost to get to the country every Sunday. Do any rambling clubs exist in your district? If so, join one.

A SHORT HISTORY OF FITNESS

The history of fitness training stretches back into the past. In 3000 BC, the Chinese invented systems of physical exercise. One was called *The Frolics of the Five Animals.* People exercised in ways that imitated the movements of animals, for example, the bear, the tiger,

the deer, the monkey, and the bird. If you think about this closely, such movements are concerned with strength, endurance, agility, speed, and grace. Our methods have not changed all that much today. In India, *Yoga* was developed thousands of years ago. It is still being practised and is, in fact, growing in popularity in Europe today. In African countries, village wrestling has been popular for as long as people can remember. The Romans built great *baths*, which provided opportunities for bathing, massage, games and exercises as well as libraries and restaurants. The Greeks invented athletics, the Olympic Games, and took a pride in the shape of their bodies. Various forms of dancing were also popular. In those days, of course, only a few people had these advantages. Most of the population were slaves and died early in life. Today we try to enable *everyone* to enjoy the benefits of physical fitness.

Project

Fitness in history

Find out as much as you can about the history of fitness and write it up in your newsbook. Draw the *Five Animals* and show what movements we can do that are similar. Discover all you can about *Yoga*. Go to your local library and find out what books they have on this subject. Can you discover anything about other forms of exercise like

Yoga? Find out all you can about the history of the Olympic Games and the training of the athletes. Do the same for Roman baths.

COMPETITIVE SPORT

When people lived agricultural lives they had enough exercise. When they moved to cities and towns, as they did rapidly during periods such as the Industrial Revolution, they needed to plan and organise fitness training. Games like football built up rules and regulations about

the numbers of players on each side and the size of the playing areas. Countries that were fittest did better in war. In our country most of the world's modern competitive games were invented and became part of the way of life of the British. People used them to keep fit and to have fun. In other countries similar developments took place. In Germany, special sports gardens were built with apparatus on which children could swing, balance, climb and jump. Over time these pieces of apparatus became the rings, bars and beams that are used in Olympic gymnastics. In Sweden other forms of apparatus were invented, and these can still be seen in many of our gymnasiums—the wall bars, boxes and small mats. The *horse* that most of us have used in physical education was once a real horse. Next it was copied in wood, and slowly it changed to the strange object we see today. At one time people actually *rode* the wooden horse to make them stronger for real horse riding. Today, we use these pieces of apparatus—ropes, benches, and other objects —to *invent* our own activities.

Today, we try to get fit by taking part in physical education, by spending as much time in the open air, walking, running, climbing, canoeing and sailing. We build sports centres where there is something for the whole family. This is happening in all countries in the world and a slogan is being shouted—*Sport for all*.

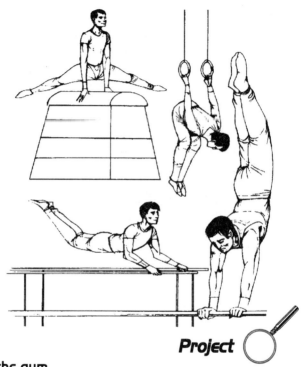

Project

In the gym

Draw all the pieces of apparatus you have in your gymnasium and try to find out their history.

What clothes do you wear for gymnastics and swimming? Find out what clothes people in other countries wore through the ages and build up a series of pictures showing the history of costumes for fitness. Make a section for this in your newsbook.

Find out which sports provide something for the family, and list the clubs and evening institutes in your district where you can get fit.

How do people in other countries keep fit? Have a page for this in the newsbook. Discover as many *systems* of getting fit as possible. Record remarks on fitness in any books you are reading.

LOOKING AT OUR BODIES

There are three basic 'types' of people—stocky, lean, and muscular. Scientists who study our growth and development call these types:

stocky	endomorphs
lean	ectomorphs
muscular	mesomorphs

It does not matter if you cannot remember these names. None of us fits any one of the descriptions exactly. We all have some fatness, some boniness and some muscularity. When you choose sports you should know something about this if you want to enjoy yourself and succeed as much as possible. Muscular people make good gymnasts and sprinters. Stocky people make

stocky (endomorph)   *lean (ectomorph)*   *muscular (mesomorph)*

good swimmers. Lean people can often run well, especially long distances. It is the same for boys and girls. You cannot change your basic type or your height, but by fitness training you can make the most of yourself.

If you start at the top of your body with your eyes, you might find out who makes the best ball players. People who can react quickly to the position of a ball, or the position of a partner, do well at ball games. Some

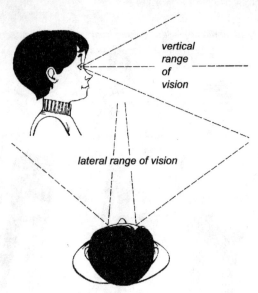

vertical range of vision

lateral range of vision

people, when looking straight ahead, can also see a long way up and down, and also to both sides. People with this ability also make good car drivers and are less likely to have accidents.

Now look at your feet. Your shoes should not cramp the toes. Your toenails should be cut properly; you should be able to curl your toes round a pencil and lift it from the floor. You should be able to walk quietly on your toes, then on your heels. If you place a blackboard on the floor and stand on it with wet feet, the marks you leave should be broad at the top and bottom but narrow in between. The feet are like the foundations of a house —they must be strong. Exercise in bare feet as much as possible.

Your muscles are arranged in pairs. Each muscle has an opposite muscle. If you contract muscle A, muscle B relaxes, and vice versa. It is easy to see this if you look at your arms. The muscle that bonds your lower arm upwards is called the *biceps*; its opposite is called the *triceps*. When you bend *biceps*, *triceps* relaxes. If it did not relax there would be no movement. One muscle would be working *against* the other. Sometimes this idea is used to make muscles stronger, and this is called *isometric* training. Perhaps you have read something about this. You will read about it later in this book. All the

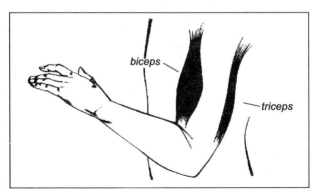

muscles in our bodies are arranged in this way. Incidentally, these names given to muscles are in Latin, the language of the ancient Romans. Really they are simple descriptions. *Biceps* means the 'two-headed muscle'. *Triceps* means the 'three-headed muscle'. Just as bicycle means 'two wheels' and tricycle 'three'.

When you exercise you can vary the effort by placing your muscles in different positions and using simple laws of mechanics. If you hang from a beam and raise your knees bent, it is easier than keeping legs straight. It is

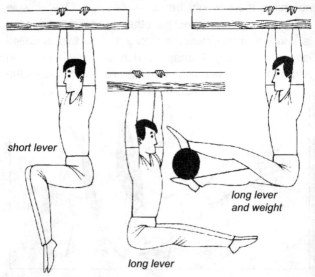

short lever

*long lever
and weight*

long lever

more difficult if you try to hold a heavy ball between your feet.

Project

Studying physique

Put the members of your class into groups—stocky, lean, muscular. Find the average height and weight, eye colours, hair colours.

Now make a list of the favourite sports of your class members. See if their choice of sports is a good one in terms of their physiques.

Next time you are walking down a street, look *straight ahead* but see how much you can recognise in the shops on each *side*, and how far *upwards* you can see. If you practise this it might improve your vision. The ability to increase your range of vision will help you be a better footballer, basketball or tennis player.

When you next have a bath, make patterns of your

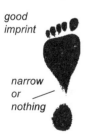

good imprint

narrow or nothing

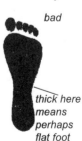

bad

thick here means perhaps flat foot

27

feet on a dark surface and see if the pattern is correct. If the shape is equally broad from end to end your doctor might find you have flat feet and give you exercises to correct this. Make a list of all muscles that you can 'pair'. Find where they start and end on your body, and what movements they control. Learn as much as you can about your body. You will live in it for the rest of your life.

By changing the 'length' of your legs and arms (by bending them) see how difficult and easy it is to do certain movements. By *slowly* increasing the difficulty you will make muscles stronger. This is called the principle of *overload*.

The way you sit, stand and move is also important. Your posture should be comfortable and graceful. Grace comes from having the head balanced properly on the spine and hips. Some scientists say that human beings were designed to move on all fours, like the dog. When we began to move in an upright position, the spine took on bends so that the various parts could be balanced easily. If these bends become exaggerated you are no longer efficient, and it is a good idea to think about this from time to time.

Have you ever thought about a good deep breath. Place your hand on your stomach and see what happens when you breath in. If the stomach tends to move outwards it is good. You are getting a really good

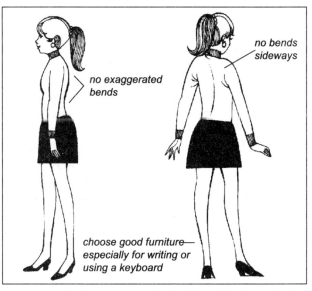

no exaggerated bends

no bends sideways

choose good furniture— especially for writing or using a keyboard

movement in the muscle (called the diaphragm) that allows the lungs to fill.

Project

Check your posture

Have a look at the postures of your friends and ask them to look at yours. If you can make a plumbline, use it. See if a straight line would go through ears, shoulders, hips, knees, feet—roughly that is. See if the spine curves unusually. Do not worry—there are wide differences between people.

Take in a deep breath *slowly*. Hold it for a count of ten and let it out *slowly*. Do this ten times when you get up in the morning, before an open window, if possible.

Lastly let us consider the heart. This is the most important organ in terms of fitness. The heart is also a muscle and is only healthy if it is used. A *healthy* heart *cannot* be damaged by physical activity. You can find out what is happening to the heart by measuring your pulse. You can find your pulse by placing a finger and thumb on the throat and you can see how many beats it makes by using a stopwatch or even an ordinary watch. The pulse is the echo of the heart as it pumps blood to all the vital

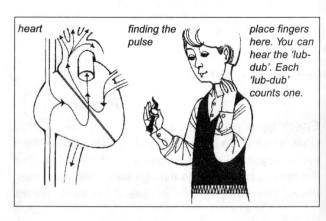

heart

finding the pulse

place fingers here. You can hear the 'lub-dub'. Each 'lub-dub' counts one.

organs of the body. When you exercise, or even get excited, the heart rate increases. If you step up and down on a bench for a minute, you will find that your pulse rate has increased. If you sit down and rest, it will return to normal. The speed it takes to return to normal is some indication of your fitness. Training can increase the speed at which this pulse rate returns to normal. Pulse rates are individual. Athletes usually have slower pulse rates than non-athletes. This is because with each beat (pumping action) more blood is pumped out of the heart by a healthy, elastic heart. With less healthy hearts, not so elastic, the heart can only respond to the demands by working faster. Heavy smoking hinders the development of a good functioning heart and lungs so if you want to be good at good sports, do not smoke.

Until about the age of twelve, girls and boys tend to match each other in terms of speed and strength. After this age, speed and strength in boys and men tend to outstrip those in girls and women. So, the world record holder in the men's 100 metres will have run a faster speed than the record holder over the same distance in the women's event. Except in a very few sports (tennis mixed doubles for example), it is rare to find men and women competing directly against each other in amateur or professional events, but, of course, there is no reason why they shouldn't in purely recreational or 'fun' competitions. And there is complete equality in the advantages of getting and staying fit and healthy.

Project

Take your pulse

Place a bench on chairs and make sure it is safely balanced. Sit on the bench and take your pulse rate, or ask a friend to do it. Then step up and down from floor to bench for one full minute. Take the pulse rate again. Rest and see how long it takes to return to normal. Take counts each half minute. At the end you can make a graph. Every week experiment exactly the same, and if you are trying to get fit, you can measure the success of your fitness training programme by the speed at which your pulse returns to normal. If it is improving then you are making progress.

PHYSICAL EDUCATION LESSONS

In your physical education lessons at school the teacher is not only trying to get you fit in a muscular sense. He or she tries to help you grow, develop, learn and enjoy yourself. You are put into different situations involving apparatus on which you jump, climb, balance, make shapes, get over, run round, use for invention, link to other pieces of apparatus. You do this in many different ways and at different speeds, with varying amounts of effort. The teacher presents you with problems that you solve in a physical way. You also learn skills that occur in games, like catching, throwing and kicking. The work you are asked to do is planned so that you will have a balanced development of your body and will enjoy vigorous exercise. It will also allow you to practise sportsmanship and friendly behaviour towards others. At the end of your school career you should have so enjoyed physical education that some physical activity will always be part of your life. You will always want to feel fit. You should be hungry for physical exercise and have had an opportunity to try many recreational skills, so that you may choose a satisfying one for your leisure time.

Most of you will, at some time in school, have learnt to dance. You should also have been taught to swim. Many of the skills you learn in physical education can be applied to your chosen sport.

Many schools today encourage students to get fit by going into the mountains to walk or climb. If you do this, go only with a skilled guide. *Never* go alone. This warning also applies to water sports like sailing and canoeing.

Project

Studying sports

This book shows you one way to compare games by putting the different skills into groups. See what other ways can be used to group and classify sports. Ask your teacher how he or she does it.

Ask yourself which sport you enjoy most and why. Compare your answers with those of others in your class.

Compare the sports activities of the boys with those of the girls. Who is best at what, and why?

Time the various parts of your physical education lesson. How many minutes for moving apparatus, how much time lost because people were talking? How many minutes actually for activity? Try to arrange your own lesson. Discuss it with your teacher. Have a page for your lesson in your newsbook.

Make models of the apparatus found in your gymnasium, and of the gymnasium itself if you can.

Find out where modern sports were invented. Use encyclopedias, general and sport, for this information.

What do you know about dance in different countries? Borrow a video camera and make a film of the dances you do at school.

Discover all you can about camping. Make your own tent.

THE STUDY OF HIGH-LEVEL FITNESS

Human beings are restless animals. They climb mountains, try to penetrate the ocean depths, attempt to fly, and are eager to reach other planets. They are keen to know just what makes them tick and the maximum achievements of which they are capable. They are always surprising themselves. Sportsmen and women are especially restless. In their constant search for efficiency, for speed, endurance, improved skill and complete concentration, they reach the limits of effort. If you can discover what it is that sets athletes apart from the average person; what distinguishes the good sportsman or woman from the Olympic champion; and whether this quality is inborn or can be acquired with training, then you are a long way along the road to explaining what is that elusive quality—fitness.

When great athletes hurl themselves through barriers of pain and fatigue to lower world running records, there are scientists waiting to measure reactions in the heart, lungs, muscles and mind. In discovering the basis of human physical efficiency, these scientists might be helping people to live longer and probably to live more happily.

In the last eighty years there has been a remarkable growth in the branch of medicine called *sports medicine*. In many countries sports medicine is well advanced. In many countries there are institutes devoted to this study, where doctors can specialise in the specific problems of injury and function in sports. In these countries the athlete, the coach and the doctor work closely together.

Olympic stadiums contain clinics where sportsmen and women can receive advice and examination. They are encouraged to have regular health checks since, in normal health, sport can have nothing but a positive effect, but if a weakness exists and is not detected, sport can cause a severe breakdown.

It is recognised now that those who administer sport, at amateur or professional level, need to bring an expert and scientific approach to their work. Athletes and those who train them are much more knowledgeable than they were in the past about how the body functions and about

how to minimise the risk of injury and long-term damage to it. It is also recognised that the mental state of someone who wants to excel in a sport is as important as physical fitness and general good health. In professional sport, the financial difference between coming first and second can be huge, and there is constant pressure to succeed. But some of the same considerations also apply to those who take part in sport for fun and who simply want to keep fit. The research that the professional game pays for can also benefit everyone else.

How do these researchers go about the business of experimenting with athletes? How can they help them? What can they learn from them? What have they done, and are they doing, on these experimental lines? Put your findings in a scrapbook.

SWIMMING

Channel swimmers are intriguing to scientists. Most people can be immersed in cold water for only a very limited period of time before collapsing. Channel swimmers, on the other hand, can swim for many hours without discomfort. One swimmer, it was found, could lie in a bath of cold water reading a book and only because he became bored with the whole business did he have to get out of the bath. Is there something special in the physical make-up of these swimmers that makes them immune from the cold? Can this something be trained? Answers to such questions as these are important, not only to swimmers, but for shipwrecked sailors, pilots who have had to bale out of their planes, and others who might find themselves tossed into water for less enjoyable reasons than trying to swim from Dover to Calais. Swimmers and doctors travelled from swimming pools to lakes conducting experiments in different climatic conditions. Sometimes the scientists acted as the guinea pigs. They decided that the decisive factor was *fat*; that good swimmers were fat athletes; that human fat was a superb insulator and that it was this surface fat that enabled a swimmer to remain warm. At the same time, they learnt much about fat. How it was laid down and taken off. In discovering something about how the body was cooled, they made some small contribution into the problems of putting people into a deep freeze for certain operations. On more matter-of-fact matters, they learnt a little about slimming and the relationship between fat and health.

While Channel swimmers are pre-occupied with retaining their body heat, marathon runners are faced with the problem of trying to get rid of it. The body tries to maintain a steady temperature. We all know the symptoms that arise if our temperature goes up, as with a bad cold.

In some experiments the athlete wears a mask with tube connections. Electrical contacts can be made from the body to electrical measuring apparatus: Heart, brain, and muscle reactions can then be measured electronically. Also, there have been great advances in the *miniaturisation* of equipment. There is, for example, a small *pill* that can be swallowed; this pill contains a tiny transistor. Once it has been swallowed, it emits electrical messages and by tuning in the research workers can understand internal mechanisms. This method has already been used in clinical medicine and in realistic experiments with sportsmen and women. The human guinea pigs soon learn that they can lose the pill in the same way that they lose a prune stone.

Sometimes a number of research organisations combine to develop the right research apparatus. During preparations for the 1952 ascent of Mount Everest, for example, it was necessary to invent a lightweight oxygen cylinder. This had to be done because all previous expeditions had failed, mainly because of the inability to control the problem of breathing at high altitudes. The Royal Navy produced a special lightweight alloy, the Air Force came up with the correct type of breathing mask, and a joint team of doctors devised means of avoiding the sicknesses that are common in mountain climbing in severe conditions.

There seems to be little relationship between pole vaulting and a flying machine, except in matters of relative height. But recent advances in developing a machine that will enable human beings to fly (without an internal combustion or jet engine that is) brought scientists into contact with pole vaulting, rowing, cycling, weight lifting and other sports. Although many centuries ago, the great artist and anatomist Leonardo da Vinci designed a flying machine, it was only relatively recently that the Royal Aeronautical Society set up a committee to explore the possibility. There are two main possibilities —a pedal-operated propeller plus fixed wing or the flapping-wing. Both demand a steady output of power.

Although human beings are capable of great bursts of power in such sports as weight lifting, they are not so efficient with regard to a steady output. In finding out just how possible, theoretically, it was for humans to fly, a number of sports were analysed, and it was found to be a realistic project. Pole vaulting was interesting because here a human being transfers his or her horizontal force into an upwards one using a simple mechanism, the pole. If people can do this, it would seem likely that they could pedal a geared propeller hard enough to fly the flying machine. Investigations into the horsepower used up in other physical activities showed it was a feasible idea, and the practical people, the pilots, got into training.

Project

The science of sport

Find as many pictures and news cuttings as you can about sportsmen and women being tested and measured by scientists. Here is another section for your newsbook.

Design simple apparatus for investigating sports activities, and think of some problems that need investigating.

Look at paintings and drawings by Leonardo da Vinci, the Italian artist and anatomist, and try drawing the human body in a similar way.

Build your own simple treadmill or stationary bicycle. These would be good for indoor training.

Project

Sport for the disabled

Do you know any disabled people? There may be ways in which you could help them to enjoy sport and fitness training. There are few sports that disabled people cannot take part in, perhaps with some modification of equipment or with a slightly different approach to the sport. Watch out for the Paralympics, the Olympic Games for the disabled, which take place just after the Olympic Games and usually in the same place. Keep a section of your book for details about the results.

The final field of experiment in this work is in rehabilitation, where the adaptation of disabled people is quite fantastic.

In Britain the International Stoke Mandeville Games for the semi-paralysed were founded after World War II, and these grew into the Paralympics movement. At these games teams play basketball in wheel chairs, throw shots and javelins, compete at archery, fencing and many other sports. A Hungarian pistol-shooting champion lost his shooting arm in an accident. Six months later he had transferred his accuracy to the other arm and was still world-class. The hammer-throwing champion, Harold Connolly (USA), suffered from what is known as Erbs paralysis of the left arm. He started hammer throwing when he was acting as 'hammer-boy' at the university track, after he found that he could throw hammers back farther than his friends could throw them forward.

These studies teach physiologists much about fitness, but they teach us all that it is the sum total of abilities in people that matter, rather than any one disability.

PART TWO

WAYS OF GETTING AND KEEPING FIT
General fitness techniques

Exercise is one of the important factors contributing to total fitness. Exercise can help to develop and maintain speed, strength, agility, endurance and skill in healthy people. Games, sports, swimming, dance activities, gymnastics exercises and vigorous hobbies, such as gardening, can all make worthwhile contributions to fitness. Exercise should be chosen according to age, sex, interest and work. Each individual varies in his or her needs. A simple slogan could be 'A daily *sweat* will get me fit and keep me fit'.

THE BATH

No one *feels* fit unless exercise sessions are completed with a shower or bath. The hot bath, followed by a cold dip and a brisk rubdown, is one of the great pleasures of life. When this can be done in the open air and the whole skin bared to the light, so much the better. In some swimming pools the Turkish bath is still available and is worth trying. The sauna bath (the Finnish hot-air bath) is also very popular and many swimming pools and leisure centres have them. All top athletes find the sauna a great

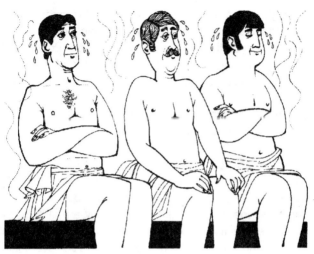

aid to training. In the sauna, the person sweats and feels better for it. The dry heat is produced by heating stones on a stove, scattering water on the stones, and allowing the wooden walls to soak up the moisture in the resulting steam. Since hot air rises, each *step* higher is hotter. You can adjust the temperature to suit your needs. Stones that do not crack under heat must be used, of course. It is possible to make your own sauna. Usually clubs and schools buy the whole sauna, or at least the stove, which today is electric. The hot bath was known to the Romans and others as an aid to fitness.

In your own bath at home you can relax in the water. You can also use the bath as a means of exercise. Stretching, curling, suppling, can all be done. The alternate use of hot and cold water to parts of the body, bruises for example, is a good form of treatment. Even for the eyes, providing it is not too hot or too cold. Give yourself a salt rubdown all over your body, followed by a shower. Salt water bathing is the magic of the sea.

MASSAGE

Massage is now very popular. Most people, especially sportsmen and women, find it extremely beneficial. You can massage your own limbs when they are stiff. Good massage is difficult, but elementary movements include stroking and kneading the relaxed muscle. All movements should be towards the heart to help the return of the blood supply. One interesting and easy form of massage is to wet a rough towel in cold water. Rinse it and then beat the limbs and joints until they become slightly red. This is often useful when joints are slightly injured.

Project

A cold shower

Take a cold shower every day for a week. If you cannot stand this, start with washing yourself with a cold flannel and see if you feel fitter.

Titles in this series:

How many different types of public bath exist in your locality? Turkish, Russian, Japanese, sauna? You might be surprised at the number.

Find out about the history of bathing, starting with the Romans, all you can about massage—there are many books available on the various different techniques.

WALKING

In the past, walking was the principal way of getting about. Today, few people walk enough but *walking is the fundamental fitness activity* on which everything else is based. In 1786, Mr Foster Powell, on the Bath Road, walked 100 miles in 23$\frac{1}{4}$ hours. In 1808, Captain Barclay walked 30 miles shooting grouse, then walked 60 miles home to complete his daily business. The following day he walked 16 miles to a dance, arrived home at 7 a.m. the next day and immediately went partridge shooting. His final event was 1000 miles in 1000 hours, and his style at the time was described as a 'lounging gait, very short steps, hardly raising the feet from the ground'.

Today the car has taken the place of the legs. But you must try to use your legs as much as possible. When you are going into town for the shopping, get off the bus two stops early and walk the rest of the way. Always walk upstairs. Do not take the lift.

Project

Ways of walking

Find out how much walking your great-grandparents did in their younger days. And your grandparents and your parents, and lastly yourselves. Compare your findings. Suggest ways in which you could walk rather than take motorised transport.

When studying history and geography, find out the walking habits of people in other countries and other ages.

Do men walk differently from women? What differences to walking do clothes and shoes make? What are the best types of shoes to wear for walking? Try walking and running in bare feet when you can and see if you feel fitter.

CYCLING

The bicycle (or 'velocipede' as it was known then) was invented in Paris in 1779. Since then, it has gone through a revolution in design, and millions of people ride a bicycle at some time in their life. It has the advantage of speed plus physical exercise. A Mrs Bloomer, who invented cycling clothes for women at the start of the 20th century, has gone into history because her name was used for an essential piece of clothing.

Danger on the crowded roads has made cycling unsafe in many areas, but as road planning improves there may be a new lease of life for the bicycle in our country. Some new towns have been built with special cycleways. In America many parks have been opened for cycle use. It might be that in the future every car owner will carry a collapsible bicycle in the boot of his or her car, which will be parked at the outskirts of all towns and the remainder of the journey made by bicycle on car-free roads.

RUNNING

Cross-country running has been the backbone of British athletics since the first days of athletics as a sport. Like walking, the basis for normal fitness, running is a fundamental *must* for any aspiring sportsman or woman. No training programme can omit running. When the running is against the clock it is a simple race.

When the training is running at different speeds across rough country, through forests, across rivers, at different speeds, it has the special name in athletics of *Fartlek* (a Swedish word that means 'speed play'). Out of running through forests in Scandinavia a new sport was born in the 1960s, *orienteering*. This combines cross-country running with map reading by compass. The most popular form of running is *jogging*. Millions of people, especially in New Zealand, where it began, and in the USA, use jogging to keep fit. Jogging is a simple run-walk system for people of all ages and both sexes, to keep the heart and circulatory system in good order.

A TYPICAL JOGGING PLAN
Monday
Total distance—2.5km (1½ miles)

Jog 100m (110 yards)   walk 100m (110 yards)   3 times
Jog 200m (220 yards)   walk 200m (220 yards)   2 times.
Jog 300m (330 yards)   walk 300m (330 yards)   2 times.
Jog 100m (110 yards)   walk 100m (110 yards)   2 times.

Tuesday
5 to 10 minute walk: easy stretching exercises.
Wednesday
Same as Monday.
Thursday
Same as Tuesday.
Friday
Slow jog for five minutes.

Jog 100m (110 yards)   walk 100m (110 yards)   2 times.
Jog 200m (220 yards)   walk 2 minutes, then rest.

Each individual must find his or her own plan. Start modestly and build up slowly.

Top sportsmen and women use *interval training*. This means running or swimming hard for short distances, resting, and running or swimming again, repeating until tired.

OTHER ACTIVITIES

Other activities that can be enjoyed by anyone, cost little or nothing and are easy to take part in are swimming, skipping, hopping and any other activity that makes the heart pump hard.

Project

Exercising

List the street or garden games that children play and that involve running and jumping. Games like hide-and-seek, and many others that are passed on from generation to generation, are useful fitness-fun activities. If there are any peculiar to your own district, find out all you can about them.

List all the safety points about cycling and bicycle maintenance.

Ask your parents if they will try jogging with you. Persuade them to keep it up for two weeks and see how they feel. You might then persuade other members of your family to take part.

When walking, walk with small steps and work hard. Do not lounge along. This will not help you get fit so fast.

Make out suggested jogging plans for the whole family, and map out those places in the country where a car owner might drive for a jogging programme.

KEEP-FIT GYMNASTICS

The *daily dozen*—a series of exercises done every day, usually every morning—is still valuable. Some time during the day a few exercises done regularly will help. Concentrate on the stomach muscles and work through the whole body, making muscles stretch their full length and then contract. Do not go quickly. Work slowly and in a systematic way. Occasionally vary the exercises. If you do them to music, you can do more and enjoy them more. Energetic dancing in front of your television set, perhaps when no one is looking, is excellent. Make sure that your spine is always supple and that you keep the neck supple. From time to time, lie flat and try to get both your mid-back and neck touching the floor at the same time. In this position you can breathe calmly and deeply to relax. Some of the simple yoga exercises are valuable, but only after instruction from a qualified yoga teacher.

You could join an aerobics class, which has the added bonus of having the company of others to keep you motivated and pubhsing yourself.

If you study the advertisements in sports books and newspapers any week, you can find many new ideas for training equipment, rowing machines, massage machines, bars for doing pull-ups, strengthening springs. You can do without them but some people find them useful.

You can think up some ideas for the daily dozen, using a broom, a towel, the chair, a duster or a bench.

Project

A daily dozen
Work out a daily dozen for yourself and your family, and draw pictures and a chart that you can follow.

Find as many books and articles on gymnastics of this kind, and make a scrapbook and a diary.

Choose pieces of music that help your gymnastic routine and build up some interesting movements.

Collect information about the special exercise machines and objects that are advertised, and put this in your scrapbook. Learn a new exercise each week.

When you complete your daily dozen easily, it means you are getting fitter. Once it seems easy, vary it. Add more repetitions of each exercise; change an exercise; do an exercise in less time. Test your increases in strength by choosing a single exercise, for example, press-ups. Keep a record showing your maximum, for the same day, and time, each week.

EXERCISING AGAINST RESISTANCE

Milo, an athlete in ancient Greek mythology, was given a calf to lift every day. The calf grew, of course, and so did Milo's strength accordingly. In the end he could lift a fully grown bull overhead.

We can work one muscle against another. This is called *isometric* training. It is recommended only for older boys and girls who are training to be athletes under the supervision of skilled coaches.

Normally we lift, not calves, but weights, specially designed to make lifting easy. Weight training is very popular but can be harmful to joints and vertebrae if carried out in the wrong way. The correct principles of lifting must be applied (page 15). Always make sure that the collars that lock the weights to the bar are tight.

You should always be supervised by a good coach, or your teacher, when you use weights.

In general there are two major ways of training with weights, for power and for endurance.

For endurance. A steady load lifted a regular number of times with repeated efforts:
9 kilograms (20 pounds) lifted ten times—rest—lift again—rest—third and final lift.

The load can be increased. The rest period can be shortened. The number of lifts can be increased.

For power. Increasing loads with decreasing repetitions:
9 kilograms (20 pounds) lifted 5 times—rest.
13.5 kilograms (30 pounds) lifted 4 times—rest.
16 kilograms (35 pounds) lifted 3 times—rest.
18 kilograms (40 pounds) lifted 2 times—rest.
20 kilograms (45 pounds) lifted once.

Again we can vary the load, the number of repetitions and the rest pauses.

Weight training should not be attempted except under supervision.

Project

Weight training

Compile a list of well-known people who have used their fitness to make a name in other careers. For example, Arnold Schwarzenegger became a film star and *Gladiators* is a popular television programme.

Write to the coach of your favourite football team and ask what resistance training they perform. Do not forget a stamped addressed envelope for a reply.

Find out what weight training is needed for athletics, swimming and other sports. See if there are any clubs, or experts, who can advise on special training like this.

Design a large chart that says, 'I will *not* be silly by working with resistance exercises alone and without guidance.'

CIRCUIT TRAINING

Circuit training is a method of achieving basic fitness and is very popular with athletes and professional sportsmen and women. It aims to develop endurance, strength, speed and determination. The emphasis is on sheer quantity of work rather than on quality of movement or skill. It is the simplest of the organised general fitness training programmes. Each activity in a circuit is simple, not requiring any special skill. Like other training programmes, however, it should first be tried under supervision and with the advice of a qualified instructor.

Here are some exercises for a circuit. Try this system for a start:

	D	C	B	A
Step-ups	15	20	25	30
Press-ups	4	6	8	10
Run	6	6	6	6
Squats	2	4	6	8
Trunk curls	6	8	10	12
Heave jumps	10	15	20	25
Bench jumps	6	8	10	12
Swing	2	3	4	5
Circuit time	10 mins.			

Method of working: the beginner performs each of the exercises in turn, completing the set number of repetitions for each exercise on the D rate. This is repeated three times, as fast as possible, with one or two minutes' rest between each circuit. The total time taken from start to finish is recorded. When the performer can complete three D-rate circuits in less than the circuit time, he or she progresses to the C rate and then to the B and A rates in turn.

If you want to invent your own circuit, choose the exercise, try each activity to a maximum, divide the maximum number by two, and this gives you a *training rate*.

Circuits can be made harder by cutting down the total time, increasing the training rate for each exercise, adding more exercises and cutting down the resting time between the three circuits.

A circuit can be invented for the gymnasium, the garden, a room, the playground, the beach, the garage —anywhere in fact. It needs little equipment but a lot of imagination.

Project

Your own circuit training

Make out a chart for yourself showing a simple circuit, and keep a record of progress over a month, a term, a year.

Design a circuit for your garden at home, your garage or your bedroom, using no special piece of apparatus, merely the normal household objects.

Use a ten minute circuit as *part* of a physical fitness schedule.

Invent some simple, but new, exercises for circuit training and some simple pieces of apparatus to make a circuit more interesting. Try circuit training to music.

RELAXATION

Although many of the preceding activities will make you feel relaxed, there are other ways of achieving this. Lie flat and breathe deeply. Listen to pleasant music, think of pleasing colours or views. Think of every part of the body from toe to head and let it go *limp* when you think of it. There are many other ways. Always relax for a short time during your training session.

Project

Ways of relaxing

Discover as many ways of relaxing as you can.

What is the effect of dance, music, swimming, games, colour, food in relaxation?

How do your parents relax after work?

Find out how top sportsmen and women relax before a big event. How do they control their nerves?

GAMES

At a basic level many sports are means to getting fit. Games like tennis and badminton, for example, are very enjoyable. They include plenty of running and jumping, and they are interesting. Many people prefer this 'play' way of getting fit, but once games players really wish to improve, they also need to follow the forms of fitness training we have been looking at.

CONCLUSION

To be best enjoyed, a general fitness programme should

be varied. It might be a good idea to have jogging twice a week, circuit training once a week and badminton once a week, with as much walking as you can manage. It all depends on your age, your energy, what it costs and your needs. If you are at a school where there is a well-organised physical education programme, you will not have time or energy for extra exercise. Keeping fit in the fresh air is best.

FITNESS FOR SPORT

Each sport has its own demands. To get fit for ball games, you need much practice using the ball and coping with situations you are likely to find in the game itself. For this reason, a form of fitness training for ball games, called *pressure training*, was developed. This means putting the player under pressure by making him or her work harder and faster than in the game itself. For example, a player is wanting to improve his heading power in football. He is surrounded by team-mates, each with a ball. They throw the ball at him in sequence, and he jumps to head it. As soon as he has headed one ball, another is on its way. It is not difficult to understand that the player gets plenty of exercise. He also gets fitter for that particular skill. Simple common sense and a little imagination will tell you how to apply this system to all the other skills of ball games.

For athletics and swimming, the interval type of training is used. Circuit training is also widespread. Throwers and jumpers use weight training and other forms of resistance training to get strong. They also work with overweight shots or discs to get stronger in their event, and with underweight implements to get faster. Each sport has its own special needs and the resistance training must suit them. This calls for some clever and creative thinking. Racket games players have also turned to systematic training of this kind since, at the top level, skill is not enough. It is the skilful player who is also fittest who comes out champion.

At a less ambitious level, sports are themselves fitness activities for everyone. At the top level, the sportsman and woman need very hard physical fitness training. He and she also need fitness training for the mind. They need confidence in themselves, single-minded dedication and devotion to their sport. For this reason, they usually need a coach who helps them not only to stick to their task more firmly but also to get the best out of themselves.

Top sportsmen and women are beautiful in their movements. They give great pleasure by their efforts and struggles, by their skills, by their behaviour, to millions of spectators. They are artists, both amateur or professional, in movement.

Project

Training for sport

In your newsbook invent and catalogue *pressure training* activities for the sports in which you are interested. Check with your physical education teacher. Try them out and see if they work.

Design some new resistance exercises and pieces of apparatus that can be used in resistance training.

You will have notes on your favourite players in your book. Make separate pages for each and keep a log showing exactly what movements each player makes during a game—how far he or she runs, how many jumps or passes are made (successful and unsuccessful), how many times he or she wins a race for the ball (or loses), and so on. In the end you will have a lot of information, and in this way you will be able to draw up a suitable fitness training programme to improve his or her play. If you know the player, discuss your findings with him or her. Ask someone to log your game like this.

Study a player who looks graceful. Try to find out why he or she makes everything look easy. Are there any points common to all graceful players? List them and discuss them with your teachers.

Write a poem or a short story about great sportsmen and women. Make paintings or sculptures based on movement in sports.

MEASURING YOUR FITNESS

Two simple tests might be useful for this:

Upward jump (power test). Stand by a wall and reach up. Mark with chalk or a wet finger where your inside hand reaches highest. Do not stretch, just reach naturally.

Swing both arms down and bend the knees (several times if you want).

Spring high into the air and reach again to make a mark on the wall as high as possible. Measure the difference between the two marks. The top Olympic jumpers and sprinters, games players, swimmers, measure over 75cm (30 ins). This test is a good one for most sportsmen and women.

Step test (endurance test). Make a bench 50cms (20 ins high), usually a gym bench on ordinary chairs is about this height. (Make sure the bench is well balanced.)

Step up with one foot. Follow it with the other. Stand up tall. Then step down with one foot. Now the other. Now both feet are on the floor. Keep this stepping action going rhythmically for five minutes or until you cannot go on any longer. Sit and rest for one minute.

Start taking pulse counts as follows:

1st pulse count (P1) from 1 to $1^1/_2$ minutes.
2nd pulse count (P2) from 2 to $2^1/_2$ minutes.
3rd pulse count (P3) from 4 to $4^1/_2$ minutes.

Find your physical fitness score by working out the following equation:

$$\frac{15,000}{P1 + P2 + P3}$$

Rough classification: over 110 excellent.

about 80 average.

Do not worry if your score is nothing like this. It could be the height of the bench, your timing, or your mathematics. There are many other fitness tests. Your teachers might know some.

Project

Fitness tests

Find out some more fitness tests from books in libraries.

Invent some simple fitness tests and try them out on your friends. See if the best games players score highly in one or two tests. See what other conclusions you can draw.

Speak to your mathematics teacher and see if fitness testing might be used in mathematics. Ask your physics teacher if a detailed study of exercises and sports might be used to understand the elements of mechanics.

KNOWLEDGE TESTS ABOUT FITNESS

See if you can answer the following test. You can if you read this book.

1 The upward jump is a test of:

    (a) endurance

    (b) skill

    (c) power.

    (Tick the right answer.)

2 In lifting weights, which are the correct instructions:

    (a) keep back straight

    (b) hold bar far away from body

    (c) use the legs as much as possible.

    (Tick the right answer.)

3 Rearrange the following words horizontally so that they are correct:

stocky	=	ectomorph
lean	=	mesomorph
muscular	=	endomorph

4 Isometric training means:

    (a) working with weights

    (b) working one muscle against another

    (c) working muscles against an immovable object

    (Cross out the wrong answer.)

Answers.

1 (c)

2 (a) and (b) are correct

3 stocky is endomorph, lean is ectomorph, muscular is mesomorph

4 (a) is wrong

PART THREE

FITNESS ORGANISATIONS

The following organisations will be able to supply information about their activities and may be able to give the names and addresses of similar organisations in your area. If possible, it is a good idea to telephone first and explain what information or advice you want. Remember to send a stamped addressed envelope when you write.

Central Council of Physical Recreation (CCPR)
Francis House
Francis Street
London SW1 1DE
Telephone 0171 828 3163
The co-ordinating body for all sports and games in the UK.

Keep Fit Association
Francis House
Francis Street
London SW1 1DE
Telephone 0171 233 8898; fax 0171 630 7936

Physical Education Association of the United Kingdom
Suite 5
10 Churchill Square
King's Hill
West Malling
Kent ME19 4DU
Telephone 01732 875888; fax 01732 875777

Ramblers' Association
1/5 Wandsworth Road
London SW8 2XX
Telephone 0171 582 6878; fax 0171 587 3799

In addition, most cities, towns and even villages have keep fit classes for people of all ages, male and female. Local newspapers often adverise these classes; the leisure department of your local authority can also help; and a local library or information centre should also have up-to-date information about them.

Larger centres of population may have several health centres and gyms (often called 'exercise studios') where people can take part in group or individual activities. It is usually necessary to pay and they can be expensive, but there is no harm in making enquiries.